MONSTERS HAVE MANNERS!

Jeff Kubiak

Braden Kubiak & Vanand

TEACHERGOALS
PUBLISHING

© 2022 TeacherGoals Publishing, LLC.
Beach Grove, Indiana

Written by Jeff Kubiak.
Illustrations by Braden Kubiak & Vanand.

All rights reserved. No part of this book may be reproduced or transmitted in any form or by any means, electronic or mechanical, including photocopying, recording, or by any information storage and retrieval system, without written permission from the publisher. For information address publishing@teachergoals.com

This book is available at special discounts when purchased in quantity for use as premiums, promotions, fundraisers, or educational use. For inquiries and details, contact the publisher.

For more books and lesson plans from TeacherGoals visit teachergoals.com

ISBN 978-1-959419-04-4 (paperback)
ISBN 978-1-959419-10-5 (hardcover)
LCCN 2023930197

Cover Concept by Amanda Fox
Book Design by Arlene Soto, Intricate Designs

First Printing 2023

QuiverVision

All black and white coloring pages come alive in Augmented Reality!

Nothing brought River more joy than monsters! River thought about them so often that they seemed real. He kept a sketchbook full of mean monster drawings. He even pretended to be a monster.

"River, please don't speak with your mouth full. Use your manners, pal," Dad said.

"Monsters don't have manners!" River roared.

"Eat your broccoli, River. It will make you strong!" said Grams.

"Monsters don't eat broccoli. It leaves stuff in their teeth," replied River, as he pushed away his plate.

"MOM! River hit me again!" yelled Summer.
"Monsters love to fight! And it was just a tap on the arm," River's face grew hot.

"River, this needs to stop—now!" said Mom. River slowly walked to his room.

"BUUUUUUUUURP!" River sighed with relief.
"River! Where are your manners?" cried Grams.
"Grams, monsters never say excuse me," said River. He burped again and patted his stomach.
"I probably shouldn't speak to Grams that way," River thought.

"I was here first, River," said Mira.

"Too bad. Monsters always cut in line!" said River.

"Pass it to me!" said River, grabbing the ball away from Manny. "Stop it, River. You can't just take it—we're teammates," said Manny.

River took the shot. "Monsters do what they want!"

At lunchtime, River went to sit with his friends.
"You can't sit here," said Manny.
"Monsters eat alone." The students laughed.

River took a seat at an empty table, head down. "At least I have my monsters to keep me company," he thought. As he flipped through his sketchbook, he noticed something: all of his monsters were alone. Just like him.

In the middle of the night, River was awoken by a voice whispering his name from the closet.
River clutched his pillow tightly. "Who's there?"

"It's Monstro," replied the voice. "And Monsterooni," said another. "And me!" "Me too!" "Hey, don't forget me!" Exiting the closet, the monsters were captivated by River's drawings on the walls. "Wow, what striking detail!" Blabs said. "It looks just like me," the monsters exclaimed one after another. "You really captured my horns," said Dome. "I love how you drew my fangs!" shouted Slash.

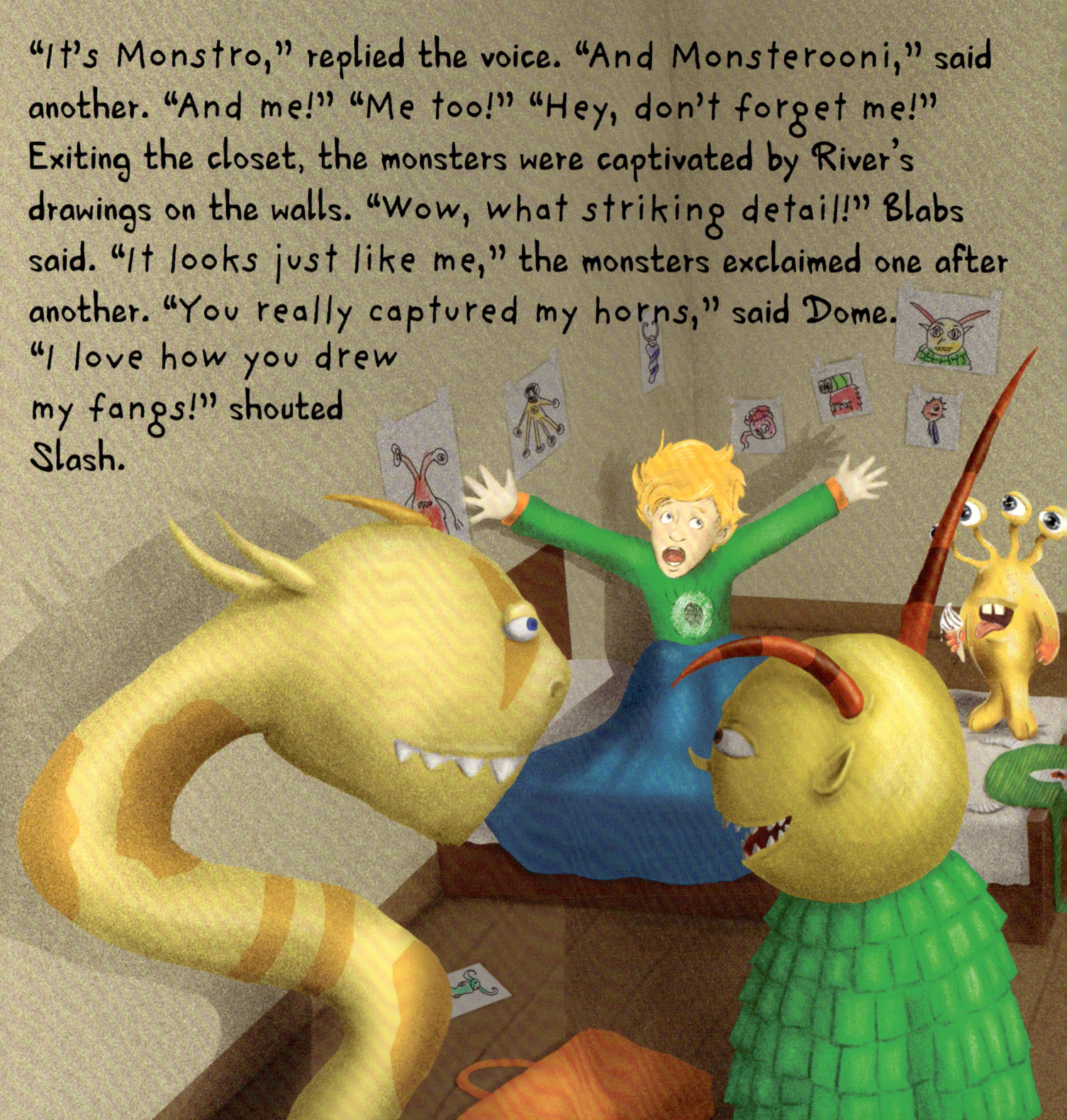

"I just wanted to be one of you," said River, trembling with fear. "But I guess I got it wrong." Tapping his head furiously, River blurted "Maybe I should start helping out at home?"

When everything was put away, Monsterooni and Slash tucked River back into bed. "Sweet dreams, River," they whispered, disappearing into the closet one by one.

"River, it's time to get up for school," hollered Dad.

River rubbed his eyes.
What a strange dream he'd had.

As River got dressed, he noticed a new drawing laying on his desk. "To our best friend, River."

A brilliant idea suddenly popped into River's mind.

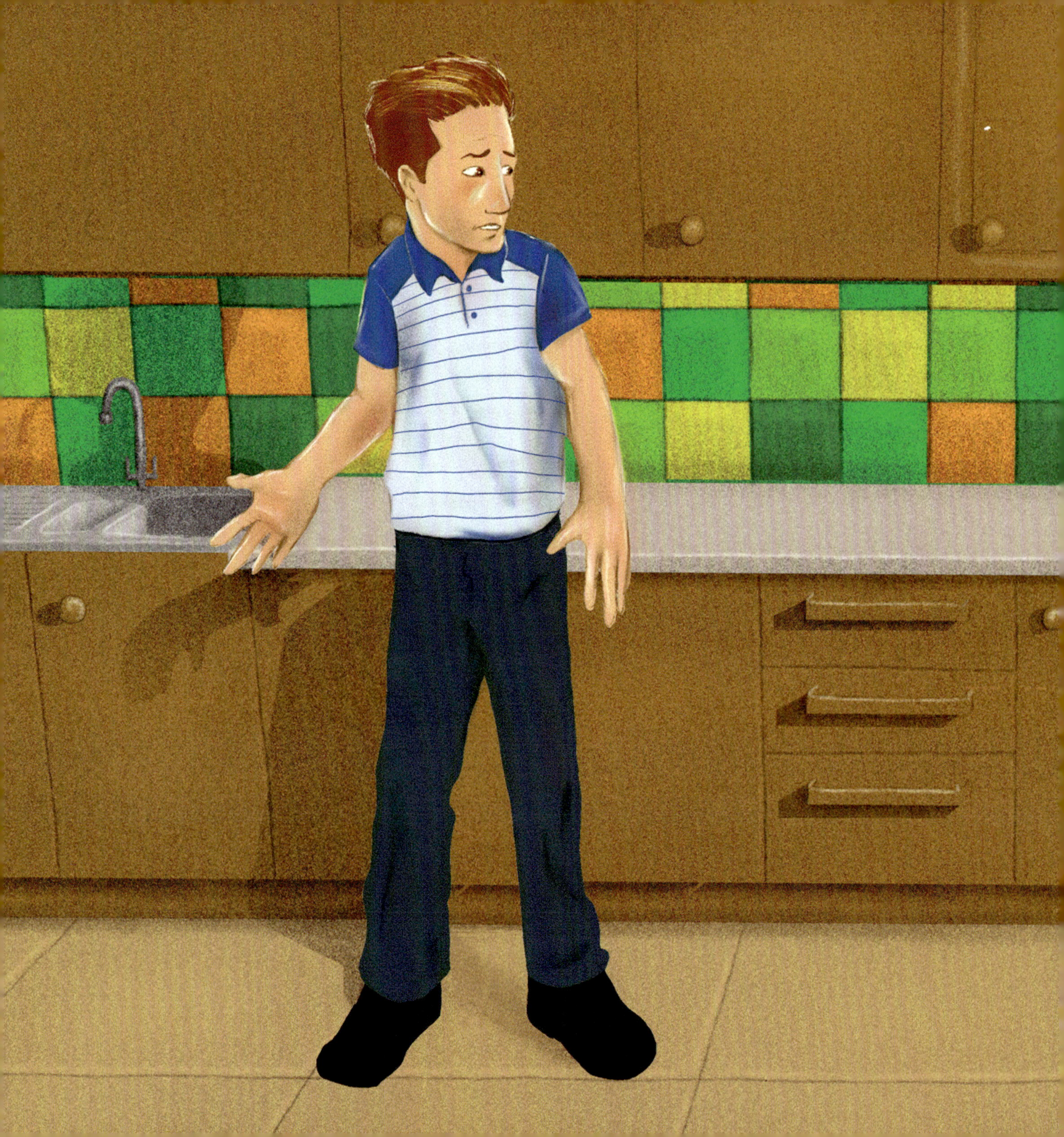

"River! You are going to be—"
"On time!" said River as he sped through the kitchen.
"Because monsters are never late."

River blasted through the classroom door, still scarfing his breakfast. He took out a marker and fixed up his sketchbook.

As he looked at the cover of his sketches, a bright grin began to grow. Because now he knew the truth: monsters DO have manners!

Jeff is an educator, author and speaker from Northern California. He taught for ten years in grades 4, 5, and 6, and now serves youth as an Elementary School VP.

Monsters Have Manners is Jeff's 3rd book, but his first project that he's worked on with his son Braden. Braden drew all of the monsters between the ages of 8-12.

Jeff lives near Sacramento with his wife Piper; daughter Keeley, and son Braden. They love to travel as much as possible, especially to areas with beaches, water, and hiking trails.

Jeff focuses his book topics on kindness, compassion, inclusion, equity and ways to help other people. He loves to travel to schools and talk about writing, literature, improving mental health, and other areas.

He can be found on Twitter @jeffreykubiak, Instagram @jeffkubiakauthor, or at jeffkubiak.com

Braden is a sports enthusiast, and plays competitive Lacrosse, and Basketball. He loves being outdoors, going to school, hanging out with his friends, playing video games, and playing sports with his dad. He's always loved to draw pictures of monsters, and is excited for his illustrations to come alive!

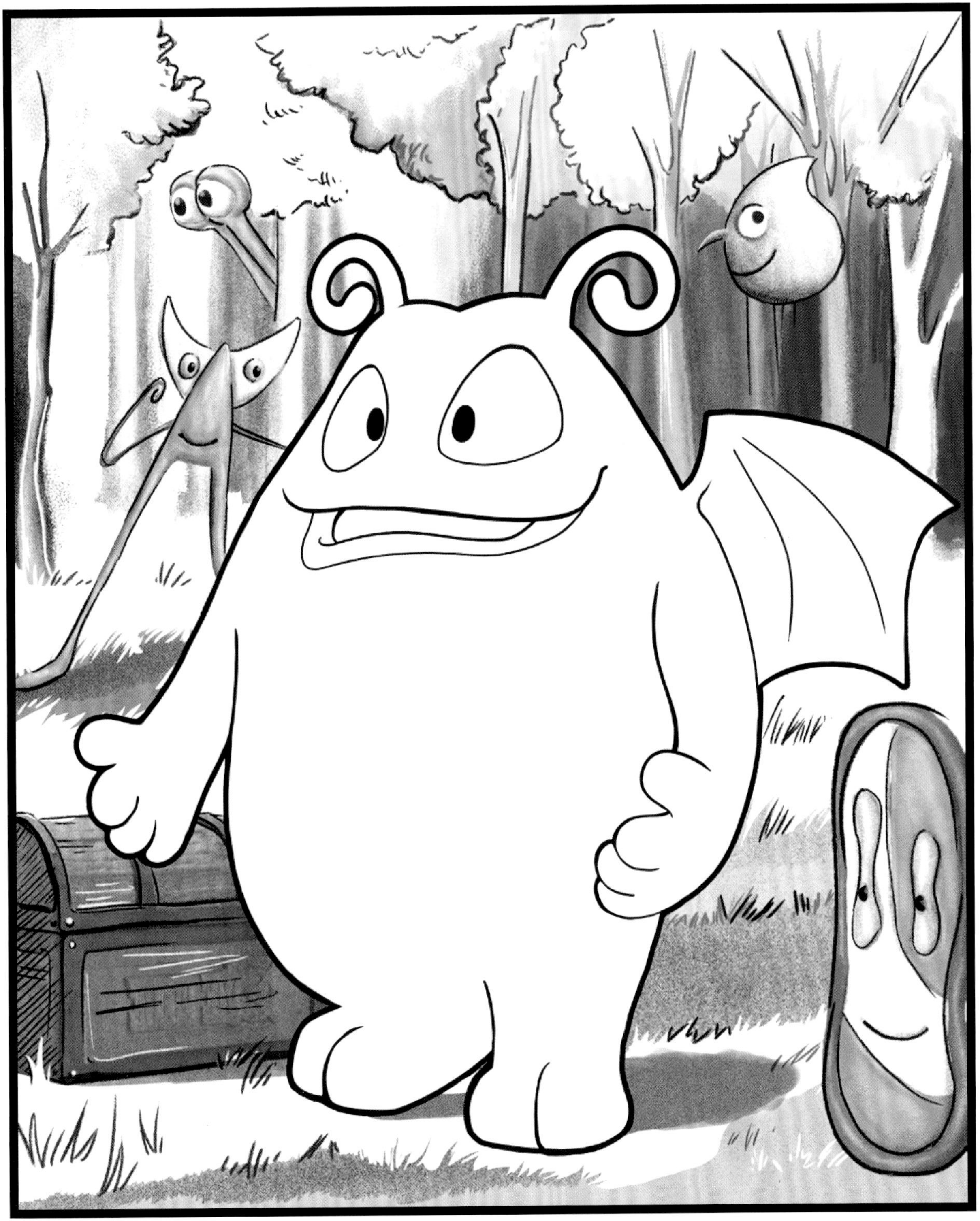